Suffering

Is My Friend
Not My Enemy

by Sharon Earnest

Cover design, book design and layout by Jim L. Friesen

Library of Congress Control Number: 2012922435

International Standard Book Number: 978-0-615-73385-2

Printed in the United States of America by Mennonite Press,
Inc., Newton, KS, www.mennonitepress.com

To Order Additional Books:
Earnest Publications
Earnestfam@aol.com

Dedication

To my dear friends, Bonnie Peacock and Carole Shuck, who like Moses, "endured as seeing Him who is invisible." They were a testimony to the heavenlies as well as to all who knew and loved them.

"For I reckon that the sufferings of this present time are not worthy to be compared to the glory that shall be revealed in us.

—ROMANS 8:18

Foreword

"The Lord wants us to embrace suffering as a friend."
— Brother Yun

"What should I speak about?" I asked the TV producer as we prepared for tomorrow's taping. "Well, I think most people would like to know what is the most important lesson you have learned in your life." Later that night I went over several possibilities in my mind, but nothing seemed to click. Then the Lord reminded me of what He said to me during a time of crisis. **"Suffering is your friend and not your enemy."** At that time suffering was more like an adversary than a friend. However, as the years progressed I found that suffering became my teacher and my friend. The lessons I learned are more valuable to me today than any amount of money.

Suffering is not a popular subject in today's church world. Unfortunately, there is a popular teaching that says it is not God's will for us to suffer. People have been taught that they suffer because they have sin in their lives, lack faith or have no understanding of God's Word. I have even heard such outrageous statements as: "The early disciples wouldn't have had to suffer, if they knew what we know today."

Elizabeth Elliot tells about a meeting with Corrie Ten Boom. The topic of suffering came up and Corrie made the following observation. "American Christians are open and eager, but they do not understand the suffering they must undergo." Recently a wise teacher said that we need to prepare people to suffer. We would all prefer to hear that good times are ahead. However, if we are honest about the days we live in, I believe we will agree with him and realize that this is a prophetic word for our time.

In order to be prepared for what is ahead we need a paradigm shift in our attitude towards suffering. Instead of our reaction being: "Why is this happening to me? It's not fair. I don't deserve this." Our response should be: "Lord, what do you want to teach me through this adversity? What do you want to do in my life? How may I glorify you in this situation? My life is in your hands."

Brother Yun, a modern day Christian who suffered greatly in China for the cause of Christ, says that our maturity as Christians depends on our attitude towards suffering. Certainly the early church had a different attitude than we have today. While working on this book I studied the lives of well-known saints: Amy Carmicheal, Jonathan Goforth, David Livingston, Charles Spurgeon, Madame Guyon, Hannah Whitehall Smith, and E.M.Bounds. They were well-acquainted with suffering. As I read their biographies I felt that I was in the presence of a holy company.

It's my desire to share with you what I learned, as I passed through the school of suffering, and from the saints who came before us. It's also my desire to encourage and equip the church to face the difficult times ahead with joy and grace. My prayer is that you too will discover that "**Suffering is your friend and not your enemy.**"

Contents

Is God in Control?

"All that comes to us is ordered by God.
To a Christian nothing is accidental."
—Watchman Nee

Shock and panic were often my initial reactions to adversity. Then I would question if God was in control of my life because it sure didn't look like it? Shock and panic are human reactions to unexpected traumas. However, I've found that as we grow in the knowledge of the Lord and His ways, we can face adversity with greater equilibrium.

It is important to settle the issue of who is in control of our lives; otherwise we will be tossed about when faced with suffering. I remembered something I read in Hannah Whitall Smith's book *The Christian's Secret of a Happy Life*. She said, "To the children of God, everything comes directly from their Father's hand, no matter who or what may have been the apparent agents. There are no 'second causes' for them." This was not written as a theory by Hannah for she had firsthand experience with suffering. However, I needed to investigate this issue for myself, and as far as I was concerned the Bible was the ultimate authority on the subject. So

I set about to study the lives of Job, Joseph, Moses and Paul who faced all types of afflictions.

Job was first on my list. I had heard so many preachers say that Job suffered because he brought it on himself. They loved to quote the scripture, "The thing that I greatly feared came upon me," and went on to say this was why Job suffered. It always grieved me when I heard statements like that. I couldn't believe that God spent forty two chapters on the book of Job just to get that point across, so I took out my Bible and started reading.

Here's what I found. There was a day when the son's of God as well as Satan came to meet with God. The Lord challenged Satan concerning his servant Job saying, "Hast thou considered my servant Job, that there is none like him in the earth, a perfect and an upright man, one who feareth God, and escheweth evil?" Satan couldn't let this go by so he countered with, "Doth Job fear God for naught? Hast thou not made a hedge about him and about all his house, and about all that he has on every side? Thou hast blessed the work of his hands and his substance is increased in the land. But now put forth thine hand, and touch all that he hath and he will surely curse thee to thy face" (Job 1:8-11).

Notice the Lord's answer. **"Behold all that he hath is in thy power only upon himself put not forth thy hand."** Then there was a second encounter between God and Satan. God boasted to Satan again about Job's integrity, but Satan challenged God saying, "Skin for skin yea, all that a man hath will he give for his life. But put forth thy hand now, and touch his bone and his flesh, and he will curse thee to thy face." Again I noticed that Satan could only do what the Lord gave him permission to do. **"Behold, He is in thine hand: but save his life."** It was obvious to me that anything that happened to Job had to go through God, the Father's hands. It was a controlled situation.

Joseph was another Biblical character that I felt I should investigate. I knew that his brothers had thrown Joseph into a pit and then sold him as a slave to the Egyptians. Not only was Joseph a slave in Pontipher's house, but he was unjustly accused and ended up in prison for 13 years. It would have been easy for Joseph to have felt abandoned by God and his dreams shattered. If we did not know the end of the story we might have questioned why this happened to him. However, it is very clear that God had a purpose in all this. Joseph made this statement to his brothers when they were reconciled in Egypt. "As for you, ye thought evil against me; but God meant it unto good. Now therefore be neither grieved nor angry with yourselves that ye sold me hither; for God did send me before you to preserve life" (Genesis 45:5). Yes, it was sin in Joseph's brothers that brought about Joseph's suffering. It was unjust, but God used it for His own purposes.

There is an interesting statement in Psalm 105:19. "He sent a man before them, even Joseph, who was sold for a servant. Whose feet they hurt with fetters, he was laid in iron: until the time that his word came, the word of the Lord tried him." This clearly says that God sent Joseph to Egypt. Our ways are not His ways for we would not have chosen the path of slavery and imprisonment for Joseph, but God had a redemptive purpose in Joseph's suffering.

How about Moses in the wilderness? Did God know where he was during those long years of tending sheep? Had I been out in the wilderness tending sheep for 40 years, I would have questioned whether God had forgotten me. But on a day chosen by the Lord, Moses saw a burning bush, turned aside and God spoke to him, calling him to deliver his people. God used those forty long years to prepare Moses to lead His people out of Egypt.

Then the Lord reminded me of Peter and what Jesus said to him concerning his denial. "Satan hath desired to have you, that he may sift you as wheat. But I have prayed for thee, that thy faith fail not,: and when thou art converted, strengthen thy brethren" (Luke 22: 31-32). This said to me that Satan had to have God's permission before sifting Peter.

I couldn't forget Paul with his long list of tribulations: imprisonment, beatings, stonings and shipwrecks. He received forty stripes five times, was in danger from robbers and wild beasts as well as from false brethren. And he was even bitten by a poisonous snake. Several of these incidents were severe enough to end his life; yet he lived into his sixties and by his own account finished his course.

What about Jesus—the greatest example of all. There were several attempts made on his life but none were successful; until in the Kiros of time He laid down his life for us. When Pilate said to Jesus, "Knowest thou not that I have power to crucify thee, and have power to release thee?" Jesus answered, "Thou couldest have no power at all against me, except it were given thee from above" (John 19:10, 11). These examples from the scripture confirmed to me that God is in charge of our lives whether it be blessings or difficulties. When we accept His control, then we can be at rest.

Carole, a dear friend of mine who suffered from Muscular Dystrophy, shared how knowing that God was in control of her life helped her to overcome her situation. Muscular Dystrophy is a debilitating disease which causes the muscles to become weak and waste away. Carole, who is now with the Lord, was limited to her bed and her wheelchair. It became increasingly difficult for her to use her right hand and her left hand was useless. She could no longer walk nor stand.

Several years ago Carole was bedridden because of a pressure sore which kept her from sitting up. Family members had to come and get her out of bed because she had no other help at that time. Carol was frantically trying to figure out what to do. The only option she thought she had was a nursing home. This was a very traumatic time for her and her mental state was shaky. God intervened in her situation, not so much with practical help but with a revelation of His sovereignty. She said she felt like He came and set her free. She knew that whatever happened to her He would take care of her. She had peace and was joyful in the midst of her tribulation. In time God provided her with health care workers, so that she could remain at home. She came to the same conclusion that Andrew Murray came to over a hundred years ago:

I Am Here
By God's Appointment
In His Keeping
Under His Training
For This Time.

When You Pass Through The Waters

*"Fear not Christian. Jesus is with thee. In all thy fiery
trials His presence is both thy comfort and safety.
He will never leave one whom He has chosen for His
own. "Fear not, for I am with thee is His sure word of
promise to His chosen ones in "the furnace of affliction."*
—C.H. Spurgeon

I was eating lunch with friends at an historic inn in Leesburg, Virginia. Ruth Catalano, a saintly old prophetess, was slated to speak to us. Most everyone there had been in her meetings before and was looking forward to her ministry. As she prophesied to the women ahead of me, I wondered what message the Lord had for me. When my turn came the prophetic word given to me was different from others. It was not glamorous or exciting. It was about hard times and afflictions.

She talked about past sufferings and how the Lord had been with me. She went on to say that the waters would not overflow me nor the fires kindle upon me. She spoke of how the Lord walks with His own through the fire and that they should not fear. I have included some of the prophecy.

"I have fulfilled my promises and will continue to fulfill them, that when thou shalt go through the rivers they shall not overflow thee, and when thou shalt pass through the fires they shall not kindle upon thee. For I am the same one that walked with those three in the fiery furnace and thou shall not fear the fires. I will keep them through the fiery furnace and I will keep them through the waters that would want to overflow and they shall come out victorious. And they shall be those who know my name and whom I know saith the Lord."

Looking back all these years later, I know the word she gave me was from the Lord. A year later my husband became ill with bacterial meningitis, was in a coma for 10 days and died. I felt like a piece of paper torn in pieces, shaken in a jar, and then dumped out on a table. My whole world was turned upside down. I was facing the frightening world of widowhood and the challenge of parenting three teenage sons without their father. Then my youngest son began manifesting severe symptoms of Obsessive Compulsive Disorder. There were rounds of tests and appointments with doctors. He suffered terribly and I found myself grieving for him, as well as my husband.

One day as I was vacuuming the twenty-third Psalm came to mind. Like many people I had memorized this well-known psalm as a child. Slowly I repeated the psalm to myself and stopped to ponder, "Yea, though I walk through the valley of the shadow of death, I will fear no evil, **for thou art with me**." Other sections of this psalm had ministered to me before, but never this passage. Now I was walking through the valley of the shadow of death.

I pictured myself in that valley, remembering the scrubby deserts I had seen in Jordan as we traveled towards Israel. It was not a lush valley. It was a wilderness. In my mind's eye I saw Jesus standing on the crest of a hill with a staff in his hand looking out over the valley. He was watching me and I knew from past experience that he would take care of me, for He was the Good Shepherd who gave His life for me. I was in that valley for two painful years. Even though there were many times when I was fearful about the future, and wondered if He was there, He never left me; He never forsook me.

Then there was the time when we lived on a tributary to the Amazon River where we were far from any help. The Lord was with me through my pregnancy, through the hardships, loneliness and lack of proper nourishment. He was with me when I left our "finca" with our lively two-year old son. (My husband had to stay behind to guard the farm.) It wasn't easy for a pregnant woman of eight months to travel seventeen hours in a dug out canoe sitting on bags of rice. Two days later I was faced with a four hour bus ride to the capital of the region followed by a fourteen hour bus ride with my son over the mountains to Bogotá. There were no cell phones and no one to protect us, but God was with us. We arrived safely without any complications to the pregnancy.

One of the most precious stories I read is of two sisters from the Lutheran Sisterhood of Mary, who were living in Israel during the Six Day War. Their house was surrounded by the Jordanian army and they were warned that they should leave the area because their lives were in danger. The sisters sought the Lord and he said to them, "Don't be afraid. I will be with you." They gathered up food and water, then moved to the basement to wait out the war.

The day came when the Israeli army invaded from the left and the Jordanian army was entrenched on the right. The sisters were caught in the middle. They spent hours in prayer. The house was shelled, and one shell dropped through the roof causing the walls of the house to collapse. Another shell landed in the house but didn't break through into the basement. Yet another shell landed on a pile of carpet and did not explode. The sisters told David Wilkerson, "In all of our years in Israel those were the most precious hours we spent because Jesus manifested Himself to us. We were never afraid. We experienced His presence as we have never known it."

There are many more stories that can be told of men and women who experienced God's presence in the midst of suffering. Brother Yun, imprisoned in China by the communist régime says that when people hear his testimony they often say, "You must have had a terrible time when you were in prison." He responds, "What are you talking about? I was with Jesus and had overwhelming joy and peace in His intimate presence."

David Livingston testified of God's presence and protection. After sixteen years in Africa, he returned to Scotland where he spoke at the University of Glasgow. By this time he had suffered twenty-seven bouts of jungle fever, the death of his wife and severe damage to an arm due to a lion attack. He asked his students the following question, "Shall I tell you what sustained me amidst the trials and hardship and loneliness of my exiled life? It was a promise, the promise of a gentleman of the most sacred honor, it was this promise: "Lo, I am with you always, even unto the end of the world." When he died they found his Bible opened to Matthew 28 and in the margin beside this verse was written, **"The word of a Gentleman."**

The Lord promises—"When thou passest through the waters, I will be with thee: and through the rivers, they shall not overflow thee: when thou walkest through the fire, thou shall not be burned: neither shall the flame kindle upon thee" (Isaiah 43:2). The saints that have gone before us testify that He keeps His word—'**The word of a Gentleman."**

His Grace Is Sufficient

"It is only through grace that we can stand till the last hour. The final celebration of the ages will not take place because of our ability to hold out through the darkness. The only celebration of the final day will be in honor of God's grace."

— ED CORLEY

I am convinced that we will not finish our course, hold onto our faith, or overcome in the midst of adversity without God's grace. My understanding of God's grace has grown as I have faced different trials. Suffering has taught me to cry out to God to receive His grace in the time of need. God's grace is not just His unmerited favor. It is His divine enablement and empowerment to face whatever situation confronts us.

There is a story my former pastor shared with us which still impacts me today. He had resigned from his church and gone to Bible school in Tulsa, Oklahoma. This was a big step of faith as he and his family could only afford to live in low income housing. At that time he had no job and no money. On the weekends he and his wife would pick up soda cans and redeem them so that they would have money for food and gas. One day he could take it no longer and cried out to God. He was feeling sorry for himself and saw no way out of his situation. Then the Lord said to him, **"Son, I don't give pity I give grace."** That changed his life and what he shared changed my life.

Earlier in my Christian walk I wanted people's sympathy, but I have learned that pity doesn't help me. I need God's grace. I need His empowerment, His divine enablement to face whatever comes my way. As I read about the life of Apostle Paul, I marvel at how he was able to finish his course in spite of so much adversity. He describes being "troubled on every side, yet not distressed, perplexed but not in despair, persecuted, but not forsaken, cast down but not destroyed." In another scripture he speaks of hungering, thirsting and having no certain dwelling place—of being persecuted, defamed and made as the filth of the world.

I personally know of no one who has gone through all that Paul went through to preach the gospel. Jesus said of Paul," I will show him how great things he must suffer for my name's sake." How was he able to endure such suffering and yet maintain his joy in serving the Lord? How was he able to keep God's purposes before him and not give up? We never see him complaining. The answer is found in I Corinthians 15:10, "But by the **grace of God** I am what I am: and his grace which was bestowed upon me was not in vain: but I labored more abundantly than they all: yet not I, but the **grace of God** which was with me."

Paul was divinely enabled by the Lord to fulfill his ministry. He learned to press into God and receive grace. Adversity can be a means to train us to press into God, to seek His face and receive his grace. Grace comes from the throne of God when we are in His presence. One of my most favorite verses is Hebrews 4:16, "Let us therefore come boldly unto the throne of grace that we may obtain mercy and find grace to help in time of need." It is in the presence of God that we receive His divine enablement to face what we must face and do what we must do.

Years ago I was in a desperate situation. We were living in Colombia when my husband and his partner decided to buy a piece of property on a tributary to the Amazon. It was a day and a half by canoe from any semblance of civilization and even further from a doctor. I was pregnant with our second child and recently had my spleen removed due to internal bleeding. It was not a good time to relocate to the jungle and I hated snakes. My picture of the jungle was dense vegetation full of snakes dangling from trees. I had no survival training and jungle living was not even on my radar. I felt this move was not the Lord's will, but attempts to tell my husband fell on deaf ears. What was I to do? I really had no one to talk to.

My parents sent me tickets to visit them in the States before we moved to the jungle. While there I shut myself up in my room and cried out to God. I was desperate to hear from the Lord, desperate for guidance, for wisdom and strength. I needed his grace to face this situation. This went on for several days and I found myself reading I Peter over and over again. I couldn't help but notice that a major theme of Peter was suffering.

Finally, the Lord led me to focus on the third chapter where Peter exhorts wives to be submissive to their husbands, giving an example of holy women who trusted in God, even as Sarah obeyed Abraham. I determined to read the account of Abraham and Sarah again. As I was meditating on what I read I thought, "Had I been Sarah, I would have been so angry at Abraham for lying and saying that I was his sister and all because he wanted to save his own life." However, I saw that even though Sarah suffered by ending up in a harem, God protected her and delivered her.

All of a sudden my heart was flooded with understanding. The scriptures in I Peter 3 were quickened to me and I knew what I was to do. I was to return to Colombia and go with my husband to the jungle. I was to submit to him trusting that God would deliver me as he did Sarah. I also knew I would probably face some suffering until the time came for the Lord to deliver me, **but the scripture illuminated unto me contained the divine enablement and power to obey the word. That word contained the grace of God and faith arose in my heart accompanied with supernatural peace.** That peace continued during the flight to Colombia and on the two day canoe trip down river to our new farm.

Life on a tributary to the Amazon was difficult and it didn't help that we had no money. We ate off the land and some of our food was not very palatable. I particularly disliked the monkey we ate when game was scarce. We lived in two rooms adjacent to a molasses mill. The floors were bamboo slats and sometimes pigs slept underneath the house. I spent most of my time cooking over a wood fire, washing clothes and taking care of my toddler. The nearest doctor was two days up river by canoe and then four hours by bus. If we had an emergency we were out of luck. I had no care during my pregnancy, but God gave me the grace to follow Peter's admonition, **"Wherefore let them that suffer according to the will of God commit the keeping of their souls to him in well doing, as unto a faithful Creator"** (I Peter 4:19). He proved Himself faithful to me. Six months after we arrived I was back in civilization awaiting the birth of my second son.

There are so many of God's saints who give testimony to God's grace and have gone through suffering much greater than I. One of them, Darlene Diebler Rose, a missionary to New Guinea experienced God's grace during imprisonment and torture by the Japanese in World War II. There came a point where she felt she couldn't go through another interrogation. She poured out her heart to the Lord. "O Lord, I just can't go through another one. I can't Lord, I just can't. Please, no more, Lord." And his reply came. **"But my child, my grace is sufficient for thee. Not was, nor shall be, but it is sufficient."**

Two weeks before Darlene was taken away by the Japanese Kempeitai, the Lord led her to memorize a poem by Annie Johnson Flint who suffered from rheumatoid arthritis. This had been set to music and she sang it often during her imprisonment. Strength would come and she was enabled to face another day of interrogation and beatings.

He giveth more grace when the burdens grow greater.
He sendeth more strength when the labors increase.
To added affliction, He addeth His mercy,
To multiplied trials, His multiplied peace.

When we have exhausted our store of endurance.
And our strength has failed ere the day is half done.
When we reach the end of our hoarded resources,
The Father's full giving is only begun.

His love has no limit, His grace has no measure
His power has no boundary known unto men.
For out of His infinite riches in Jesus.
He giveth and giveth and giveth again.

I no longer fear what may come my way because suffering has taught me that "His grace is sufficient." I know now that I can tap into that limitless supply of God's grace whenever I need it. I can proclaim with Darlene Diebler Rose, **"Oh, the eternal, ever-present, undiminished supply of God's glorious grace!"**

Warning! Harden Not Your Heart

*"Keep your heart with all diligence; for out of
it are the issues of life."*

—PROVERBS 4:22

I have found that there is a temptation to harden one's heart in the midst of adversity. The writer of Hebrews warns us to be careful how we respond to trials and tribulations. "Harden not your hearts as in the provocation, in the day of temptation in the wilderness" (Hebrews 3:8). Satan is watching our reactions and responses to misunderstandings, injustices, disappointments and adversity hoping that he can fan the flames of bitterness and resentment.

One of my biggest challenges was over the printing of my husband's novel. I had already faced many battles before the novel was ready to be published. Every 3 or 4 months I would inquire about the progress of the book and was assured that it would be finished in a few months. This would go on year after year and at a critical point the translator declared that she was quitting. Finally, after years of struggle, the work was completed and the publisher e-mailed me with the good news that the book would be finished in time for a book fair in Bogotá.

I made plans to travel to Colombia for the unveiling of the novel, picturing myself signing books from eager buyers. Instead I received the shocking news that the publishing company did not have enough money to print the book. This was after I had invested considerable money for editing and translation. I was told that if I wanted to pay for printing costs, they would print it; otherwise, it wouldn't happen. I was devastated and felt like I had been hit by a two by four. Years of suffering and sacrifice had been put into this project and now I had no idea how I would ever see the novel published.

This unwelcome news came right before I was to speak in several churches in Colombia. I was devastated, angry and frustrated. I did not feel like teaching or speaking. I knew that I had to do something about my heart's condition. I could not let a contaminated heart keep me from meeting my obligations. I had to hear from the Lord or I would have nothing worth sharing. **And in order to hear clearly I needed a cleansed heart.**

By that time I had learned to deal with a contaminated heart. I had a mentor, a pastor, who suffered misunderstanding, false accusations and persecution. I shall always be grateful to him for what he taught me. One thing the Lord made very clear to me through his ministry was that it does not matter what someone does to you, whether it is right or wrong, just or unjust. What matters is whether your heart is free from contamination. I stopped focusing on what people did to me and focused on my reactions to the situation.

I knew I had to do something about my response to this huge disappointment, or I wouldn't be able to fulfill my commitments. I shut myself in my room and started praying. "Lord, I am so disappointed and angry. This has been such a long battle to see this book completed. I feel let down and betrayed and I sure don't feel like speaking in the next two weeks. Lord, please wash me and cleanse me. Cleanse my heart with the blood of Jesus. You said, 'If we confess our sins you are faithful and just to cleanse us from all unrighteousness.' I need cleansing right now. I need your grace to forgive, Lord. I want to have a pure heart. I can't stand for my heart to be contaminated. I don't want anything to come between us, Lord. Oh Lord, help me!"

After a real battle in the spirit I overcame the disappointment and anger. The Lord cleansed my heart and not too long afterwards, He provided another publisher for me. What has been made clear to me is that we live in a war zone. "The whole world lies under the sway of the evil one" (I John 5:19). It is a fallen world and not everything that happens to us is just, fair or good. Our enemy, as Peter says, is like a roaring lion seeking whom he may devour. So he is watching us, hoping that the next time we experience disappointments, hurts, or injustice, we will become bitter, hard of heart or nurse a grudge. He is counting upon a root of bitterness to spring up and defile us. If that happens, he has just won the battle. "Looking diligently lest any man fail of the grace of God; lest any root of bitterness springing up trouble you, and thereby many be defiled" (Hebrews 12:15).

I call this basic warfare—Warfare 101. This is where we can win or lose the battle on a daily basis. If we allow our heart to become contaminated and hardened we cannot hear from God. And when we cannot hear from God, we are in trouble for "we live by every word that comes from the mouth of God." We are then no threat to the enemy, have no authority and our faith has been contaminated. The just shall **live** by faith. "Faith comes by hearing and hearing by the word of God" (Romans 10:17). If Satan can keep us from hearing we will have no faith to pray, preach, or confront the enemy.

Another thing I have learned about the need to keep a cleansed heart has to do with people. The scripture clearly tells us that, "We wrestle not against flesh and blood, but against principalities, against powers, against the rulers of the darkness of this world, against spiritual wickedness in high places" (Ephesians 6:12).

Most of our offenses come through people and often through our family, friends, church members or co-workers. It is very important to step back after an offense and remind ourselves that we are not fighting with flesh and blood. Many times people are yielding to negative spirits and we receive the brunt of their anger, jealousy and injustice.

Suffering has taught me to be ruthless with myself and not allow any anger, bitterness, or feelings of injustice to remain in my heart. I run to the Lord and ask him to cleanse me from my wounds, all resentment and anger. This does not mean that I do not deal with a wrong situation, but if the Lord permits me to confront a person; I must do it with a cleansed heart and a humble spirit. I need to give myself time to go before the Lord and see the situation from His perspective.

Keeping my heart cleansed is one of the most important ways I win the victory over Satan. I am declaring the cleansing power of the blood of the lamb. I am declaring, "If we confess our sins He is faithful and just to cleanse us from all unrighteousness." There is power in the blood of the Lamb. There is cleansing power. And He who has shown grace to me when I was undeserving gives me the ability to extend grace to others.

"And the blood of Jesus Christ his Son
cleanses us from all sin."
—I JOHN 1:7

Redemptive Purpose

*"And we know that all things work together for
good to them that love God, to them who are
called according to his purpose."*
—ROMANS 8:28

I was attending a conference in Colombia, S.A. where one of the
speakers, a young man from Venezuela, was talking to the women.
He was well educated, with several degrees, a psychologist, pastor
and teacher. He considered himself an expert in many fields and was
busy impressing us. After touching on several subjects he started
pontificating about Romans 8:28, "All things work together for
good for those who love the Lord and are called according to his
purpose." "You know this isn't always true," he stated with great
authority. "People have interpreted this wrongly. This can't be
true in every case," he stated emphatically, making his case by giving graphic scenarios of people who had been brutalized, maimed
in tragic accidents, or parents whose children had been murdered.

It was all I could do to keep from jumping up and shaking the
young man. I wanted to say to him, "You don't know what you are
talking about. You are too young and inexperienced, you just don't

know how God operates," but I restrained myself. It has been my experience after walking with the Lord more than 50 years that all things do work for our good. In other words, He can take failures, tragedies, sufferings, adversities and use them for our good and for His glory.

For instance, there were the six months I spent in the jungle. At the time I couldn't see anything redemptive about it at all. Once God delivered me from that life I was determined never to return to Colombia again. It was six months of deprivation, loneliness and hardship. I could see no fruit from that experience. However, years later I finally understood that God had a redemptive purpose for my time in the jungle. First of all, my husband was writing a novel which took place in Colombia when he died. There were five or six chapters to complete and I was the only one who knew how it should end. The last part of the book took place on a tributary to the Amazon where we lived. Because I experienced life there, I was uniquely equipped to finish the novel.

Secondly, while there I suffered as the poor Colombians suffered in that region. We had no money and lived off the land. I had to live as they lived—wash clothes in the river, cook over a wood fire, eat a diet of corn, rice and wild game. There were no fresh vegetables, fruits nor any extras that we like to eat. I could relate to the Colombians struggling to make a life for themselves and identified with them. Years later when the Lord took me back to Colombia, I often shared my jungle story and there was an instant rapport with my audience.

There was also a redemptive purpose in our marriage. My husband had gone to the jungle knowing that I was not in agreement. After our time there he announced, "If we are going down a river we are going to paddle in the same direction." In other words, we would not make a move without knowing that we were in one accord. This was a principle that we operated on for the rest of our married life.

It is true that tragedies happen to Christians. The scripture does not say that all things are good; it only says that God works all things together for good. It is not a good thing when a child is hit by a car and killed, or a when a soldier is badly maimed by a land mine, or when our parent's retirement savings are wiped out by fraud. It did not seem to be a good thing when Amy Carmicheal fell into a pit crippling her for the rest of her life, or when Joni dove into the pool and broke her neck.

We can all agree that none of the scenarios above are what we call good. But I have discovered that God will take everything and work it for our good and His glory, when we offer our suffering to him to be used for His purposes in our lives and others. Dr. Moon of Brighton, England is a wonderful example of this principle. He found himself stricken with blindness. He could no longer do the things he had done before, but he offered his blindness to the Lord. This is what he prayed. **"Lord I accept this talent of blindness from Thee. Help me to use it for thy glory that at thy coming thou mayest receive thine own usury."** Then God enabled him to invent the Moon Alphabet for the blind, by which thousands of blind people were enabled to read the Bible. Many of these people came to know the Lord and were saved.

When I read Dr. Moon's story I was awed by his response to suffering. Instead of giving into self pity and bitterness he saw his blindness as a gift. As someone said, "suffering will either make us bitter or better." We may not understand why we are suffering. We may not see any redemptive purpose in our sorrows, but in time it will be revealed to us. Dr. Moon probably was unaware in the beginning how his gift of blindness would bring God glory, but later he had the joy of seeing his prayer answered above all that he could ask or think. Today his Moon Alphabet continues to bless thousands of blind people.

I doubt that Joseph understood the purposes of God when he was thrown into a pit and sold as a slave, then falsely accused and imprisoned. But in the end he was able to say to his brothers, "Do not therefore be grieved or angry with yourselves because you sold me here: for God sent me before you to preserve life" (Genesis *45:5*). As Hannah Whitehall Smith said," God made the wickedness of his brethren the chariot that carried Joseph to his place of triumph."

Job did not understand the heavenly battle that he was involved in, nor did he see any redemptive purpose in his suffering: the loss of his children, his animals, his goods and later his health. Job struggled but he continued to trust God. When my husband died unexpectedly Job's words came to me. "Naked I came out of my mother's womb, and naked I shall return, the Lord gave and the Lord has taken away; Blessed be the name of the Lord." Of one thing, I am sure, there will be thousands upon thousands of people in heaven waiting to see Job and thank him for his faithfulness. They will tell him how his trust in God in the midst of suffering strengthened them. I will be one of them.

One of the most famous examples today of redemptive suffering is in the life of Joni Erickson Tada. When she dove into the swimming hole and broke her neck, it seemed that any meaningful existence was over for her. She would spend the rest of her life in a wheelchair dependent on the care of others. But when she offered herself to God, He worked in her life in a miraculous way. As we look at her accomplishments today, we marvel. She is a painter, writer, singer, speaker and missionary to the handicapped around the world. In all of these pursuits she testifies to the goodness and the grace of God.

Even if our enemy Satan causes our suffering, God will use it for redemptive purposes. I like very much what Johannes Facius says about the difficulties Paul experienced from the messenger of Satan. "These difficulties produced much glory for God and promoted His kingdom because of the grace poured out in ever increasing measures in Paul's life. In the end, the messenger of hell who bothered Paul would have regretted his actions as he discovered that he had been the instrument in producing the grace through which Paul led thousands of people to the Lord." I would like to add that countless millions have been edified and blessed for two thousand years by Paul's prison epistles. I am one of them.

At the time of our sorrows and suffering we don't see that it has any redemptive purpose. However, if we will offer our suffering to the Lord and ask Him to use it for His glory, He will answer our prayer. He will do above and beyond what we can ask or think, just as he did for Dr. Moon. If you haven't offered your suffering up to the Lord I would invite you to do so now.

"Father, you know the suffering I am going through and even though I don't understand why or see any purpose in it, I offer it up to you. Lord, you said in your word that you would use it for good. Lord, I ask that this suffering be used for your glory just as you did in the case of Dr. Moon and that you bring good out of it. May my suffering be used to help others and may I be able to comfort others with the same comfort that you have comforted me." Amen.

"Blessed be God, even the Father of our Lord Jesus Christ, the Father of mercies and God of all comfort, who comforteth us in all our tribulation, that we may be able to comfort them who are in any trouble, by the comfort with which we ourselves are comforted of God"
—II CORINTHIANS 1: 3, 4

Living By Every Word That Comes From The Mouth Of God

"The only way to go through tribulations is to have an ear to hear what the Lord is saying and then to obey His word."

—JOHANNES FASCIUS

When we go through suffering we have two choices. We either turn to God and seek His face or we turn away and blame Him for our circumstances. Many times our normal channels of help are cut off. Doctors do not have the answer, our friends can't help us, our families don't know what to do and as we found out recently the government can't help us. In times like this we desperately need to hear from God. After forty years of wandering in the wilderness Moses said to the Israelites, "He humbled thee and suffered thee to hunger, and fed thee with manna which thou knowest not, neither did thy fathers know; that He might make thee know that man doth not live by bread alone; but by every word that proceedeth out of the mouth of the Lord doth man live"(Deuteronomy 8:3).

Jesus tells us that without Him we can do nothing. In the midst of suffering we find ourselves vulnerable, weak, cast down and dependent. In the world's eye this is a catastrophe, but in the eyes of the Lord this is good. He is training us to depend upon Him and Him alone. I have certainly found this to be true in my life. It seems that I keep learning this lesson at a deeper level each time I face adversity.

In the days ahead we can no longer depend upon our thoughts, ideas and wisdom. We need to hear from the Lord. We need His wisdom. We need His guidance. As Johannes Fascius said, "The only way to go through tribulations is to have an ear to hear what the Lord is saying and then to obey His word." One thing is certain; we are more inclined to cry out to God and wait for a word from Him when we are suffering. This is His way of disciplining us so that living by His word becomes a way of life.

When I passed through the maze of my sons' illnesses, I desperately needed to hear from God. Sometimes I needed a word of comfort, a word of courage, a word of wisdom, a word of direction or a word to strengthen me. The Lord was faithful. My part was to take the time to seek Him daily and wait upon Him. My part was to come unto the throne of grace to receive grace and mercy to help in the time of need.

One day the Lord brought I Corinthians: 10:13 to my mind. "There hath no temptation (trial) taken you but such as is common to man, but God is faithful who will not suffer you to be tempted (tried) above that ye are able; but will with the temptation also make a way to escape, that ye may be able to bear (endure) it." The main emphasis given to this scripture was always, "God will not give you more than you can bear." But I saw a part of the scripture I had not seen before, "the way of escape that ye may be able to **endure it.**" The Lord spoke to me that the way of escape is His word that He quickens to us. His word gives us the grace to endure the trial set before us. His word contains His power to overcome in the situation. I do not need sympathy when I am facing adversity. I need His grace and His grace often comes through the scripture that is quickened to me.

Our very lives may depend upon living by every word that comes from the mouth of God. Darlene Diebler Rose, a missionary to New Guinea during World War II, tells of a time when the Japanese invasion was imminent. She and the missionaries she was with were faced with a difficult decision. Should they stay and face certain suffering or be evacuated with all the foreigners on a Dutch ship. Dr. Jaffray, their leader, gave this advice, "Go to your knees and say, Lord, what do You want me to do? Shall I go or shall I stay? This is extremely vital," he said, "because then no matter what happens in the months or possibly years that lie ahead, you will know you are exactly where God wants you to be. If He leads you to leave, you'll never feel that you were a coward and fled. If you are led to stay, no matter what happens you can look up and say, Lord, you intended for me to be right here." After much prayer all the missionaries said that it was the Lord's will to stay. Three days later, the ship that they were to take was torpedoed and sunk. There were no survivors.

Darlene goes on to say that it is imperative that we learn to follow the Lord when He speaks. "We must be obedient no matter what He says to us, it may even mean our lives." This is a good example that God's ways are not our ways. Human wisdom would have said yes, we must leave. The Japanese are closing in. We must leave before they get here, but God knowing the future was watching over His children.

Brother Yun, known as The Heavenly Man, tells how his second imprisonment in China was due to not obeying the Lord. The Lord gave him a dream and his wife warned him, but he said, "Look, the time for harvest is almost upon us. Let us wait a few days, then we'll go." He said that the Holy Spirit even spoke to him through Matthew 2:13, "Get up. Take the child and his mother and escape."

Yun did not listen to the warning because he said he had been operating in his own strength for months. Pride had sprung up in his heart and instead of obeying the Lord, he based his decisions on human logic and his own wisdom. Even his co-workers had warned him not to stay at home, but he didn't listen. Four days later plain-clothed PSB officers ambushed him outside his house and arrested him.

Sometimes suffering is a result of warfare. In this case we certainly need to hear from the Lord before we go out to confront the enemy. If we fight in our own strength, using our own wisdom, we are doomed to failure. One of the outstanding characteristics of David was that he did not depend on his own wisdom. He understood how important it was to hear from the Lord. When he went to battle he sought the Lord. I have learned that I need to do the same.

It does not do any good to start slinging scriptures at the enemy, if I have not heard from the Lord. They have no power and come with no authority and will not hit the target. Johannes Fascius warns us, "We can pick all the Bible verses we like and try to throw them after the enemy, but if the word was not given to us by the Spirit for any particular situation, it won't work. The dynamic divine faith we need to overcome the enemy comes by hearing the word from the Spirit, not just picking a word from the scriptures."

Jesus is the best example we have of how to fight the enemy with the word of God. He did not pick just any scripture to use against Satan. He was led by the spirit into the wilderness and we can be sure that he was led by the Spirit in his choice of scriptures to counter Satan's attacks. And it was he who said to Satan, "Man does not live by bread alone but by every word that comes from the mouth of God."

Spiritual experiences come and go, but when God gives us a word we can stand upon it no matter what storm comes against us. We can fight the good fight of faith with the word the Holy Spirit quickens to us. His word, our daily bread, is God's grace to us and contains the power and wisdom of God. It is a lamp unto our feet and a light unto our path.

> *"Remember the word unto thy servant, upon which thou hast caused me to hope. This is my comfort in my affliction, for thy word hath quickened me."*
> —PSALM 119: 49, 50

Brokenness

"It is not until a beautiful kernel of corn is buried and broken in the earth by death that its inner heart sprouts, producing hundreds of other seeds or kernels. And so it has always been, down through the history of plants, people and all of spiritual life. God uses broken things.
—THOMAS TOKE BUNCH

It is clear from the scriptures that God delights in the man or woman who has a broken and contrite heart. "The Lord is nigh unto them that are of a broken heart and saveth such of a contrite spirit" (Psalm 34:17). I believe that some of our suffering is engineered to bring about brokenness. We must be delivered from our own self sufficiency and become completely dependent on the Lord.

Moses is a prime example of one who experienced brokenness. Raised in the king's palace, we see Moses as a confident man, a man used to authority, and one who takes matters into his own hands. He sets about to deliver his people by his own strength which results in the murder of an Egyptian. Forced to flee from the wrath of Pharaoh, Moses ends up in the land of Midian where he tends sheep in a dry and barren wilderness.

God has to remove him from Pharaoh's palace to bring about brokenness and prepare him to lead the Israelites in the wilderness. Forty years later when God appears to Moses in a burning bush, we find a changed man. He is no longer self-confident, in fact his reply to God's command is, "Who am I that I should go to Pharaoh and that I should bring the children of Israel out of Egypt." Also Moses tells the Lord that he is not eloquent and is slow of speech and tongue. All self-confidence and self-reliance has gone. That is exactly what God needs in a leader.

Johannes Facius, a well-known writer, teacher and leader in intercessory prayer, tells how the Lord spoke to him about brokenness after he went through three years of deep depression. He said the first thing the Lord spoke to him after bringing him out of a dark tunnel was the following: "Johannes, all along this way you have been walking I have been longing to extend to you my healing touch, but I could not do it until you had been utterly broken before me. **For in the days to come I cannot use you the way I have planned and give you my anointing in an increasing measure unless I know that your spirit is broken and your heart is contrite. I will not entrust my power and the heavy anointing of my Spirit to anyone who has not been broken.**"

I believe that the Lord allows us to fail at times so that we learn to depend totally upon Him and have no confidence in ourselves. Johannes Facius says that we do not need more self-confidence as is often taught today, but a Christ-consciousness. He says that the Lord allowed him to be humiliated in front of his friends around the world at a conference in Jerusalem. It was so that he would know in the future that it was only the Lord that worked through him. Only the Lord would get the glory.

I think of Peter who was so cocky, so sure that he would stand with Jesus in his trial; yet he denied him three times. What looked like a colossal failure in Peter's life, God used to bring about a brokenness and dependence upon the Lord. As we read first and second Peter we no longer see the brash and bullish Peter but we see a humble and broken man. He writes in his greeting in II Peter, "Simon Peter a bondservant and apostle of Jesus Christ" and later, "God resisteth the proud, but giveth grace to the humble. Humble yourselves therefore under the mighty hand of God, that He may exalt you in due time" (I Peter 5:5, 6). He also says, "Wherefore let them that suffer according to the will of God commit the keeping of their souls to Him in well doing, as unto a faithful creator" (I Peter 4:19).

It seems to me that God has been teaching me brokenness throughout my life. I remember the first time I went to Colombia as a missionary. I was young, naive and untested. My attitude was something like: "Here I am Colombia!" But God was saying, "Here I AM Sharon. I am going to do a work in your life, a work that will bring about brokenness and a dependence upon me." My first five years in Colombia were not nearly as glamorous as I had envisioned. They were filled with hardships, adversity, misunderstandings, illnesses, one of which resulted in a serious operation, and a stint in the jungle. I did not understand why all this was happening. I only knew that my only choice was to look to the Lord.

What was one of the Lord's objectives when he led the children of Israel through the wilderness? It was to humble them, to make them dependent upon the Lord. In the past they had been dependent upon Egypt. "And he humbled thee, and suffered thee to hunger, and feed thee with manna which thou knowest not, neither did your fathers know, that He might make thee know that man doth not live by bread only; but by every word that proceedeth from the mouth of the Lord doth man live"(Deuteronomy 8:3).

What is God's objective in our lives? Is it not to humble us and make us dependent upon Him? I believe that when the Lord unrolls the canvas of our lives we will thank Him for those times of disappointment, failure and adversity. We will see how God has used them to break us from self-confidence and pride.

Pride is deadly. God resists the proud. Paul tells us that he was given a thorn in the flesh, lest he be exalted above measure by the abundance of revelations that he received. We do not know what the thorn was but we do know that Paul prayed that the thorn be taken away. The Lord answered him as He answers us many times, "My grace is sufficient for thee, for my strength is made perfect in weakness." Therefore, Paul says, "Most gladly therefore will I rather glory in my infirmities, that the power of Christ may rest upon me" (2 Corinthians 12:9). Paul went from a confident, educated, esteemed man to one whose only confidence was in Christ Jesus. He put no confidence in his flesh.

Watchman Nee says to understand the Lord's purpose is to see very clearly that He is aiming at a single object, the breaking of the outward man. "If we will open our eyes to see that everything which comes into our lives can be meaningful and that the Lord has not wasted one thing, we can receive suffering with the right attitude. With the right attitude we can offer our suffering to the Lord that He might bring about the needed brokenness in our lives."

There is an interesting story about Arabian horses. They are horses that are chosen to carry the king. However, before they are ready for this great work they must be trained and disciplined. Day after day they are taken through their paces until the ultimate test comes. They are taken out into the desert and driven for several days until they come to an oasis. Of course, they are excited and eager to satisfy their thirst. Then as they reach the water they are ordered to stop. Those that obey and wait to drink are chosen to carry the king. Those that do not wait are disqualified. We, like those horses, are chosen to bring glory to the King of Kings and the Lord of Lords. We can only do this as we yield to the disciplines of the Lord, as we are humbled and broken, as we glory in Christ Jesus and have no confidence in the flesh.

There is a poem by a civil war soldier that expresses to me what

God is doing in the life of one who yields to the Lord and allows Him to prepare him to bring glory to His name.

I asked God for strength that I might achieve.
I was made weak that I might learn humbly to obey.
I asked for help that I might do great things.
I was given infirmity that I might do better things.
I asked for riches that I might be happy.
I was given poverty that I might be wise.
I asked for power that I might have the praise of people.
I was given weakness that I might feel the need of God.
I asked for all things that I might enjoy life.
I was given life that I might enjoy all things.
I got nothing that I asked for but everything I had hoped for.
Almost despite myself my unspoken prayers were answered.
I am among all people most richly blessed.

—Unknown

"We can only be strong in Him when we are weak in ourselves. Our weakness therefore is our greatest strength."
—HANNAH WHITALL SMITH

Loving God When He Only Gives Suffering

*"I had only to learn a very deep lesson, to drink
the cup to its bitterest dregs; and now I am thankful
that I passed through the hard school, which teaches
you the highest love, love towards God even when
he gives nothing but suffering."*
— SABRINA WURMBRAND

Shortly after I left the jungle I was given the book *The Pastor's Wife*, by Sabrina Wurmbrand. Her husband Pastor Richard Wurmbrand was imprisoned by the Communist for 14 years. During her husband's imprisonment Sabrina and her son experienced great hardships, including three years Sabrina spent in slave labor camps. She endured back breaking work, freezing weather, starvation rations and lack of sleep. The last few months of her imprisonment she was forced to work at a pig farm where her job was to shovel manure. The pig sties were ankle-deep in liquid filth and a vile nauseating stench permeated the whole area. Even her clothes, her hair and the food she ate reeked of the foul odor. During this time she fell into despair and in her heart cried out to God, "My God, my God, why hast thou forsaken me?"

Fortunately, her tenure at the pig farm did not last a long time and Sabrina was eventually released. She said that she had to learn a deep lesson which teaches you the highest love—love towards God even when He gives nothing but suffering. When I read those words I wept. In my heart of hearts I knew what she said was true and her words comforted me for I had been in the school of suffering for several years. At the time I did not understand why I had to pass through so many afflictions. I could see no purpose in them. I could only submit myself to the Lord and trust in His infinite wisdom.

Today if we quoted Sabrina we would be assaulted by Christians from every side. "How can that be? God is a God of love. He wants to bless us. If she just had faith!" In the last few years the emphasis has been on blessings. "Come to the Lord and He will bless you, give and you will be prosperous." Even today I heard a well-known preacher teach about claiming the seven blessings of Jubilee. God does bless us. He loves us, but He desires a love that is greater than a love which is based on His gifts to us.

Dr. A.W. Tozer, pastor, writer and former editor of *The Alliance Witness*, wrote about The Three Degrees of Love. The first degree is that of gratitude for what God has done for us. "I love the Lord **because** he hath heard my voice and my supplication." We love Him, **because** He first loved us." I love Him **because** He has answered all my prayers. Many of our praise songs have this element in them. There is nothing wrong with these songs, but as Dr. Tozer points out this is an immature love. I am afraid that this is where we find many in the church today.

Some have moved on to the second stage of love where we love God for His glorious being. We love Him for His character, His faithfulness, His mercy, His longsuffering and because He is a righteous and just God. However, there is still a "because" in our love. An example of this is found in the Song of Solomon where the bride admires her beloved. "My beloved is white and ruddy, the chiefest among ten thousand. His mouth is most sweet; yea, he is altogether lovely." Dr. Tozer describes this love as a love of excellence. We love Him for His greatness

The third stage of love is a mature love. This is the same love that Sabrina Wurmbrand experienced. It is the love that Job exemplified. It was not dependent on God blessing him as he had in the past. Job's love was a love that had no **because** attached to it. In the midst of his suffering he proclaimed, "Though He slay me, yet will I trust Him." There was no **because** in his love. Dr. Tozer says that the higher type of love does not give reasons for loving. It does not say, "I love because," it only whispers, "I love."

Dr. Tozer gives a wonderful example of love that has no **because.** Picture a mother of a child who is brain damaged and unable to communicate with the parent. There is no laughter, no response, no ability to communicate love and no excellence in the child to admire. There is no reason to love the child, yet the mother loves the child. **Mature love needs no reason to love.**

As I meditate on the third stage of love I believe that the early Christians exemplified this love. Their love for God was not based on receiving blessings. They did not love God for what He could do for them. They loved Him even when He gave them only suffering. I think of Peter and Paul and the many saints since then. Their love was a mature love.

Madame Guyon was one who demonstrated a mature love towards God. She loved God in spite of the sufferings in her life. In her twenties she suffered an unhappy marriage, persecution from her mother-in-law and the death of her children. In her later years she was misunderstood, maligned and persecuted. Finally, she was imprisoned for 10 years and spent four years in the infamous Bastille. During her imprisonment she was ill, suffered painful maladies and endured a period of great desolation when everyone seemed to be against her.

I couldn't help but be deeply touched by her response to her dire situation. She wrote, "The stones of my prison looked in my eyes like rubies; I esteemed them more than all the gaudy brilliance of a vain world. My heart was full of that joy which You give to those who love You, in the midst of their greatest crosses." This was a woman who loved God with a mature love. Later she wrote this poem while she was locked away in the Bastille in France.

Strong are the walls around me
That hold me all the day;
But they who thus have bound me
Cannot keep God away:
My very dungeon walls are dear,
Because the God I love is here
They know, who thus oppress me,
Tis hard to be alone;
But know not, One can bless me,
Who comes through bars and stone;
He makes my dungeon's darkness bright
And fills my bosom with delight.

Thy love, O God, restore me
From sighs and tears to praise;
And deep my soul adores Thee,
Nor thinks of time or place;
I ask no more, in good or ill,
But union with Thy holy will.

Tis that which makes my treasure,
Tis that which brings me gain;
Converting woe to pleasure,
And reaping joy with pain,

Oh, tis enough, whatev'er befall.
To know that God is All in All.

I have come to the conclusion that suffering purifies our love towards God. We are moved from loving Him for what He can to do for us, to loving Him no matter what circumstances come our way. We no longer love Him for His goodness alone nor for His blessings, but love Him no matter what He permits in our lives. I believe that the Lord wants to move the Church today from an immature love to a perfect love—One that knows no **because**. One that says:

> *"Although the fig tree shall not blossom,*
> *neither shall fruit be on the vines; the labour of the*
> *olive shall fail, and the fields shall yield no meat:*
> *the flock shall be cut off from the fold, and there shall be*
> *no herd in the stalls: Yet I will rejoice in the Lord,*
> *I will joy in the God of my salvation."*
> —HABAKKUK 3:17

Poem used by permission of Christian Literature Crusade from the book Madame Jeanne Guyon.

Having Done All To Stand

Ten days before I was to leave for Colombia I felt a tingling sensation in my right leg and then my knee began to hurt. By the next day the pain was so severe that I was forced to go to the emergency room. My first thought was that it must be time for knee replacement surgery. I didn't waste any time getting an appointment with a specialist. While examining me he noticed a rash on top of my knee and stated that he couldn't operate on me in that condition.

A trip to my regular doctor didn't help much either. She was puzzled by the location of the outbreak. She said it looked like shingles, but couldn't be sure because this dreaded malady usually attacks the trunk area of the body. I was given some cream and pain medication and sent home. A few days later another doctor looked at me and after much deliberation came to the conclusion that I had shingles. By this time it was too late to take medication. I would have to let shingles run its course.

What followed was a long tormenting illness that left me unable to work. I was in constant pain, for shingles affects the nerves, and could not sleep for more than one or two hours at a time. I spent most of my nights watching "Home Improvement," "Flip That House,' and "Clean Sweep." After two weeks I was a wreck. I've had some serious health problems in the past but nothing as debilitating as shingles. I found it hard to concentrate, read my Bible or pray. I felt old and useless. Paul's description of "cast down but not destroyed" described my situation at the time. Because I could do nothing, just barely hold on, I was tempted to feel as if I was of no value to the Lord.

The only thing I could hear from the Lord was, "**Maintain Your Position.**" I remembered reading a statement by a missionary to China who was imprisoned during WWII. She said that ninety per cent of spiritual warfare is standing—remaining firm, or as Paul says in Ephesians 6, "Having done all to stand." That was what the Lord was requiring of me. The purpose of the enemy is to move us from our position in Christ during times of adversity. Standing is maintaining our position in the finished work of Christ. The Greek verb stand means "hold your ground." It is a military term. We are called to hold our ground, to maintain the victory that Christ has already won for us.

We are in a wrestling match against principalities and powers. "For we wrestle not against flesh and blood, but against principalities, against powers, against the rulers of the darkness of this world, against spiritual wickedness in high places. Wherefore take unto you the whole armor of God that ye may be able to withstand in the evil day, and having done all, to stand" (Ephesians 6:12).

The battle I faced in the midst of enduring shingles was over my position in Christ. Was I justified by my performance or by the performance of Jesus Christ? It was not about what I do or don't do, but about what Christ has done. The position I needed to maintain was, 'The just shall live by faith." I am justified by faith in what Christ has done. He is my righteousness. I don't have to meet the criteria of the world. It's not based on my ability to perform. I stand complete in Him.

Martin Luther is a wonderful example of one who maintained his position in Christ, or held the ground of victory which Christ had won. After years of struggling and searching Luther's eyes were enlightened to the truth of the gospel. "The just shall live by faith." It is faith in Christ alone that justifies us. This was a truth that Satan kept hidden from the church for hundreds of years. Luther took a stand when he was put before the Catholic Church Council and the German Princes. He was challenged to withdraw the 95 thesis that he had nailed to the door of the Cathedral. His answer to them was, "I cannot and I will not retract anything, since it is neither safe nor right to go against conscience. I cannot do otherwise, **here I stand, may God help me, amen.**" And he stood enduring death threats, persecution, intimidation and ex-communication. But he was unmoved. His bold stand changed the world forever.

Job is another example of one who stood his ground. Job was the subject of a heavenly battle. Satan challenged God saying that Job only worshipped Him because God blessed him. God allowed Satan to touch his possessions and family, yet Job said, "Naked I came into this world, naked I go out of this world, blessed be the name of the Lord." And later when Job was covered with boils he continued to maintain his position. He continued to trust in God and to worship the Lord even though he didn't understand why this was happening to him. By maintaining his position he was affecting the warfare in the heavenlies; he was winning a battle in the heavenlies.

The church of Jesus Christ is called to hold the ground, to maintain her position in Christ. I think of a church in Colombia where one of their members, a precious young man, was killed in a most horrible way. This was an opportunity for this small congregation who had already faced adversity to throw up their hands and quit, but they looked to the Lord for His grace to carry on. They held their ground.

Sometimes it seems as if we are about to be pinned to the ground. I have felt that way many times as I faced different adversities. But when I cried out to the Lord He gave me His grace to stand firm and not be moved. Most of the time His grace came through a scripture that He quickened to me. I think one of the best things we can do when we see our friends and loved ones blown about by the winds of adversity is to pray for them to receive a word from the Lord. Special experiences are wonderful, but don't last. However, a word from the Lord is like a solid rock. It gives you something to stand on and not be moved from your position in Christ.

Elizabeth Elliot tells of a time shortly after her first husband Jim Elliot died. She woke up one morning in the jungles of Ecuador to a heavy downpour of rain. The river had risen dangerously and she was overwhelmed by the thought of packing up, getting into a dugout canoe with her daughter and traveling on the river all day long. She says she was lonely, desolate and trapped, but she looked up to the Lord. His word to her was, "**Lo I am with you all the days. All the days, no matter what the weather, or how total the isolation.**" She took heart and did the next thing, which was to pack up and get herself and Valerie into the canoe. It rained all day, but it didn't matter for the weather in her soul had cleared up. By God's grace she maintained her position. She did not give in to discouragement. She stood firm.

Nehemiah is a wonderful example of one who stood firm in the midst of attacks from the enemy. Nehemiah answered the call to rebuild the wall in Jerusalem. When his enemies found out what he was about to do, they conspired to get him to quit. In other words, they tried to move him from his position. Their first weapon was ridicule. "What do these feeble Jews? Will they fortify themselves? will they revive the stones out of the heaps of the rubbish which are burned? Even that which they build if a fox go up, he shall even break down their stone wall" (Nehemiah 4:2). In spite of their taunts, Nehemiah looked to the Lord and continued his work.

Then they plotted to hinder the work. Again Nehemiah prayed to God and set a watch against them day and night. Finally when Sanballat and Gershem heard that there was no breach left in the gate, he sent word to Nehemiah saying, "Come let us meet together in one of the villages." Notice Nehemiah's response. **"I am doing a great work, so that I cannot come down, why should the work cease?"** And later there were threats but Nehemiah did not move from his position. He had a course set before Him by the Lord and he was determined to finish it.

Now after more than 50 years of walking with the Lord, I realize that our position will be challenged many times over the course of our lives. It will come in many different ways: an illness, sorrows, persecution, disappointments, betrayals and problems. No matter the circumstance, we are called to stand in the evil day and having done all to stand. The wonderful news is that He will enable us to stand against the wiles of the enemy. If we look up to the Lord, He will send His word of Grace. He will send His divine enablement and we like Job will be a testimony to the heavenlies.

Therefore, let us take seriously the admonition from the book of Hebrews. Hebrews was written to a group of Christians who were in danger of being moved from their position, their faith and trust in Jesus Christ.

"Let us hold fast the profession of our faith without wavering: for he is faithful that promised."
—HEBREWS 10:23

Perseverance

"Therefore I have set my face like a flint."
—ISAIAH 50:7

It may seem strange to say that suffering has taught me perseverance. Perseverance was not a natural trait of mine. I was one of those who were bursting with excitement when the Lord inspired me to start a project, until I was attacked by discouragement. The first time I moved to Colombia, I had all sorts of glorious visions about what I would do and expected that this would happen rather quickly. Instead, I found myself teaching music at the Official British School and later doing everyday kinds of things like cooking, washing dishes, and cleaning at the retreat center my husband started. It was the type of work that demanded persistence day after day. There was nothing glamorous at all about the work we had to do. It required perseverance.

When I undertook the task to finish my husband's novel, I was in for a long battle. Although I always dreamed of being a writer, I knew little about writing a novel. God blessed me with a writer friend who patiently went through the book with me. First I had to do a lot cutting—first time writers always write too much, then

I had to travel to Colombia to do some research. The hardest part came when I finally got a publisher. Years dragged by while I waited for work to begin on the translation, and when it did there were all sorts of problems. It was out of my hands. All I could do was pray. Year after year, I was told that the book would be ready. Then came the time of unveiling only to be told they couldn't afford to print it. So I had to find another publisher. Finally, nine years after the death of my husband the book was published.

There is a scripture about Abraham which says, "After he had patiently endured he obtained the promise." There is a time lapse between the promise and the receiving of the promise. With Abraham it was 25 years, with Moses it was 40 years in the wilderness, with Joseph 13 years before his dream was fulfilled, and David spent many years as a fugitive before he became King. This required perseverance. Many of our dreams are aborted because we do not persevere. We give up just before the answer comes.

I've learned that one of the reasons we have to wait is that God is battering us into shape, so that we might be made ready to fulfill our calling. I have come to see that what is being worked out in us during the time of waiting is almost more important to God than the answer. He is teaching us and preparing us as we are being shaped and refined. Oswald Chambers says, "God gives us the vision, then He takes us down to the valley to batter us into the shape of the vision and it is in the valley that so many of us faint and give way." He goes on to say, "Every vision will be made real if we have patience."

I think we have problems with patience today because we live in a microwave society. We are used to getting what we want now. We read about famous Christians who seem to have it all—large ministries, TV appearances and books on the best seller list. We do not see, however, the day of small beginnings in their lives, the years of patiently waiting and the battering into shape that took place before they received the promise.

As I write this book I am reading about the lives of many well-known saints who persevered. There is William Wilberforce who labored over 30 years to see slavery abolished in England. And William Carey, missionary to India, who labored for seven years with the Bengali people without one convert. It is said if ever a man had cause to give up it was Carey. In 1812 a warehouse fire destroyed his grammar books, dictionary and a whole version of the Bible that he had translated. Yet Carey knelt and thanked God that he had strength and started all over again. Most of us would have given up.

I love the words of Paul and I often read them when I am feeling weak and ready to quit. **"But none of these things move me,** neither count I my life dear unto myself, so that I might finish my course with joy, and the ministry, which I have received of the Lord Jesus to testify the gospel of the grace of God" (Acts 20: 24). Beatings did not move him, nor imprisonment, stonings, hunger, thirst, danger or betrayals. He persevered. He had a purpose, a goal and that was to testify to the grace of the Lord Jesus Christ. He was like a runner who had a race to finish.

English missionary Gladys Alyward is a wonderful example of one who persevered against tremendous odds. Gladys, a parlor maid, felt called of the Lord to be a missionary to China but all the doors seemed closed to her. Her education was limited and she did poorly in Bible school. As a result the China Inland Mission would not accept her. Heartbroken, but undaunted, she went to work as a house maid and saved enough money to buy a train ticket to China by way of eastern Europe and Russia. She set off with two bags, one with her clothes and Bible and the other with a small stove and some food. When she arrived in Siberia there was a war going on and Gladys was forced to leave the train and walk two days in the snow to Gita.

When she arrived in Gita she had problems with the authorities. One of her bags was stolen and she was sent to Vladivostok where they planned to whisk her away to work as a machinist in Siberia. God intervened through a young woman who advised her to take a boat to Japan. Even though she had no money, the captain had mercy on her and took her aboard. When she arrived in Japan she found missionaries who gave her food and shelter. One of them exchanged her train ticket for travel to Tientsin, China.

Gladys finally arrived in China, but soon found that her troubles were not over. She was informed that Mrs. Lawson, the missionary she was to meet, lived 23 days away in a remote part of China. At this point I would have questioned if I had heard from the Lord, but not Gladys. She did not quit and the Lord provided her with funds and a guide for most of her trip. Gladys arrived at her destination, but Mrs. Lawson died a few months later and Gladys had to continue alone. The rest of her story is a testimony of her perseverance and the Lord's provision and protection. A movie has been made about how she saved the lives of 94 children leading them over the mountains to escape from communist invaders.

Another missionary who is an example of perseverance and God's enabling grace is Jonathan Goforth. Jonathan like Gladys was a missionary to China. As I read his biography I was awed by his steadfastness and perseverance. After he came to China he and his wife experienced a fire which destroyed their possessions, the death of five of their children and the Boxer rebellion where many missionaries were killed. They had to flee for their lives and Jonathan was attacked by a mob with clubs and swords. Even though Jonathan had an open wound at the back of his head, he continued on. He refused any offer of help. He only asked that they would pray that the Lord will give him strength as long as he had work to do.

These traumatic experiences during the Boxer rebellion did not deter Jonathan and his wife from returning to China. They later faced danger in Manchuria where they lived and evangelized. They were threatened by bandits and for a period of time had a bag packed in case they had to leave on short notice. During Jonathan's later years he was plagued with carbuncles, fevers, colds and pneumonia, but kept pressing on. Even blindness did not stop him. With all the strength he could muster and in spite of his disability he continued to proclaim the gospel and to speak for the cause of missions.

Jonathan Goforth, Gladys Alyward, and William Wilberforce all had a race to run. We too have a race to complete. I have come to see how important it is to persevere so that we may finish our course. When I am tempted to be discouraged and give up, I think of the saints who have gone before us. I meditate upon Jesus, "the author and finisher of our faith; who for the joy set before him endured the cross, despising the shame and is set down at the right hand of the throne of God" (Hebrews 12:2).

In my imagination I hear James Frazier say, "I will not, by God's grace, let anything deter me from going straight ahead in the path to which He leads." I hear the great cloud of witnesses surrounding us shouting, **"Don't stop, don't quit. Persevere; run with patience the race set before you. Finish your course. Because He endured you can endure!!"**

When Suffering Is The Result Of Warfare

"He teacheth my hands to war; so that a bow of steel is broken by mine arms."

—PSALMS 18: 34

During most of our suffering our call is to stand and not be moved by the circumstances around us. However, there are times when suffering is the result of an attack by the enemy. Then we are called not only to stand but to fight. God teaches us the principles we need in the midst of the battle to confront the enemy. I have been up against a foe far greater than I; therefore, I needed God's help, His strategy and His wisdom. Psalm 18:34 says, "He teacheth my hands to war, so that a bow of steel is broken by mine arms." I have leaned upon that promise many times and He has been faithful to instruct me and give me discernment and direction.

James Frazier's biography *Mountain Rain* has been a great encouragement to me. A missionary to China in the early 1900's, he endured suffering as a result of a satanic attack. He was living in a place which he called the Lisu Hilton Hotel, a rundown hut made of bamboo and thatch, perched on the side of a mountain. Two thousand feet below him was a roaring river and all he could see as he looked out were mist covered mountains.

James had been working with the Lisu for some time praying, preaching and teaching Christ to a large number of them, but they did not seem to be interested. A deepening gloom fell over James. At first he thought it was due to his isolation and loneliness. Then he wondered if it was the poor food or perhaps the never ending days of mist and rain. Gradually he became aware of a soul destroying influence. Doubts assailed him. Questions came to him again and again. "Your prayers are not being answered, are they? No one wants to hear your message. The few who first believed have gone back, haven't they? You see, it doesn't work. You should have never stayed in this area on such a fool's errand. You've been in China five years and there's not much to show for it, is there? You thought you were called to be a missionary; it was pure imagination. You'd better leave it all, go back and admit it was big mistake."

James wrestled with doubt and suicidal despair several times. The powers of darkness had him isolated and if they could get to him now, they could put an end to the work. After several days letters arrived and in one was a copy of *The Overcomer*. He read it over and over. "What it showed me," he said, "was that deliverance from the power of the Evil One comes through definite resistance on the ground of the Cross." In humble dependence upon the Lord he talked to Satan using the promises of the Scripture as weapons. And they worked!

I understand what James went through for I have faced similar attacks during missionary work in Colombia. That same message and voice of doubt attacked me. I recorded one incident I had a few years ago. The Lord had given me a specific assignment to accomplish. I began to experience great resistance in my spirit accompanied with a strong desire to go home. Thoughts assaulted me disguised as my own. "You are wasting your time, you aren't doing anything, accomplishing anything. You are only a woman. This is a job a man should do. Maybe you missed it on this trip. They don't want to hear you. It will be boring to them."

I have been encouraged as I read about James's battle with principalities and powers. There is a lot we can learn from him. I noticed that James said that he resisted Satan in humble dependence upon God. I have learned that we cannot win a battle if we think we know what to do. We must submit ourselves unto the Lord. The scripture says, "Submit yourself therefore unto God. Resist the devil, and he will flee from you" (James 4:7).

Our safety lies in humility and dependence. Francis Frangipane says that Satan is terrified of humility, because humility is the surrender of the soul to the Lord, and the devil is terrified of Jesus Christ. Notice the attitude of Jehoshaphat who feared and set himself to seek the Lord when he was being threatened by Moab and Ammon. "O our God, wilt thou not judge them? For we have no might against this great company that cometh against us, neither know we what to do, but out eyes are upon thee" (2 Chronicles 20:12).

Jehoshaphat and the people humbled themselves before the Lord and came to him without any plans or ideas of their own. When Jehoshaphat said, "We do not know what to do but our eyes are upon you," he was articulating his dependence upon the Lord. Many times the Lord brings us up against something greater than our abilities so that we learn to depend upon Him. Jehosphaphat needed to hear from God. He needed His direction, His strategy and His encouragement. He needed a wisdom that comes from above. The Lord answered him and gave him direction, encouragement and instructions.

Jesus is our model for warfare. He was led by the Spirit into the wilderness and led into battle. When Satan came to attack Him his plan was to get Jesus to move from His position—to take things into his own hands—to depart from his mandate to give his life for mankind. Thank God Jesus stood firm and resisted Satan with the sword of the Spirit which is the Word of God. He resisted Satan with the Word, but not just any word. It was a word quickened by the Spirit of God.

When I am attacked by the enemy I need to hear from God. I need a rehma word; just the right word sent by God. As James Frazer said, we need different scriptures or truths at different times. Jesus spoke the specific word needed in His case and Satan had to flee. We want to hit the target and not just shoot arrows all around the dart board. We need a specific word for a specific situation. The Lord showed James that he was to resist Satan based on the ground of the cross. James used specific scriptures based on Christ's victory at the cross to overcome Satan.

If we have the right attitude we can learn a great deal when we are in a battle. As we wait upon God for wisdom and direction, He will teach our hands to war. The Holy Spirit will quicken the truths needed to fight the enemy. And then He will anoint our prayers and declarations as we pray and declare the truths needed to fight our enemy. We will find that what we learn in the midst of our suffering will lead us to victory just as James Frazier was led in Christ's train of triumph, a triumph finished and complete.

> "Now thanks be unto God, which always causeth us to triumph in Christ, and maketh manifest the savour of his knowledge by us in every place."
> — 2 CORINTHIANS 2:14

A Testimony To
The Heavenlies

*"When a young mother in her wheelchair perseveres
through loneliness, when an elderly widow keeps
leaning on Christ, when Christians in dark corners
of the world hold onto God's grace, the entire spiritual
world stands on tiptoe, wondering, how great their
God must be to inspire such loyalty!"*
— JONI ERICKSON TADA

Several years ago a group of intercessors traveled to the geographical center of the United States, which happens to be in Kansas. We were there to support John Hamrick and his wife Martha, who were fulfilling the call of the Lord to pray in the capitals of all 50 states. It was a daunting task, but they were determined to obey the Lord and to intercede in each capital as the Lord led. As we prayed for the nation I saw in my mind's eye something like a satellite dish pointed toward the heavenlies. The Lord showed me that the church had a responsibility to penetrate the heavenlies with the knowledge of God.

What I saw was confirmed in Ephesians. 3:10. "To the intent that now unto the principalities and powers in heavenly places might be known by the church the manifold wisdom of God." Many people ask me what it means to make known the manifold wisdom of God. Johannes Fascius gives the best explanation that I have found so far.

"We are not just here to be a testimony to secular society. We exist as the Church for God's purposes within the spiritual realm. And what He needs us for is this; that everything He accomplished in Christ Jesus on the cross may be displayed in its full reality."

One of the most important ways we do this is in our responses to trials and tribulations. We need to realize that our lives affect more than just the people around us. We are called to prove, to demonstrate, to display all that Christ accomplished on the cross in its full reality to principalities and powers in heavenly places. We are called to show to be true, to validate, to establish the truth of Christ's redemptive work. And what more effective way to do this than in the midst of our greatest challenges and tribulations.

Edith Schaffer's book *Affliction* gives a wonderful example of how we can affect the heavenlies, even in the midst of the kind of suffering which renders us useless. The Schaffers had a dear friend Mr. Van Der Weiden, who had been diagnosed with advanced stage brain cancer and given a few days to live. He had been a great supporter of their work at L'Abri and had just taken tea with them a few days before they received the devastating report. Edith and Francis left immediately for Holland to comfort their friend. As they stood around his bed he said to them, "Before—I everything could do. Now—I nothing can do." Edith said that he was referring to the many occasions when he had been active in arranging discussion groups at the university and at his store.

As Edith stood there looking at the distress on their friend's face she had a flash of illumination. She saw that the next hours and days would be the most important ones of his life—a part that he could still have in the battle in the heavenlies. She said that when Satan attacks believers, he is trying to put a barrier between an individual and God the Father. He is attempting to get people to curse God as he did with Job, to blame Him for their troubles and to stop loving God. So Satan attempts to attack God through one of his children. The victory is won against Satan when God's people continue to love Him and trust Him in the midst of unchanging circumstances.

What Edith said to Mr. Van der Weiden had a deep impact on me. **"You still have your most important work to do now, as you face the temptation to spend your remaining hours in wishing it could be otherwise, or blaming God. Instead of that, you tell God you really trust Him implicitly and love Him in the midst of this circumstance. No one else has this particular portion of the battle to take part in, nor this particular victory to win for the Lord."**

As I pondered what Edith Schaffer told her friend, I thought of Job as an example of one whose response to afflictions affected the heavenlies. Satan was sure that Job would curse God after he lost all his possessions and his children. He accused Job before God of only worshipping God for the blessings he received from Him. However, in spite of all his losses, Job continued to worship God. He declared, "Naked came I out of my mother's womb, and naked shall I return thither; the Lord gave, and the Lord hath taken away; blessed be the name of the Lord" (Job 1:22).

Satan did not give up after he lost the first battle to get Job to curse God. He tried a second time challenging God by saying, "Put forth thine hand now, and touch his bone and his flesh, and he will curse thee to thy face." So Satan went forth and smote Job with boils from the bottom of his feet unto the top of his head. Even Job's wife said to him "Why don't you curse God and die?" In spite of his agony Job never turned against God. Finally, he declared," Though He slay me yet will I trust in him"(Job 13:15).

Our reactions to our trials have the potential to affect the heavenlies and make known to principalities and powers the manifold wisdom of God. We can demonstrate, show to be true, and validate everything Christ accomplished at the cross. The manifold wisdom of God is all those wonderful truths surrounding Christ's death, burial and resurrection. They are the truths concerning the victory that Christ won at the cross and our position in Christ.

The Lord showed me how my sufferings could affect the heavenlies. One morning my sister-in-law called and as we were talking she said, "I just don't understand why you have to deal with three sons with serious disabilities and do this without the support of their father." She was genuinely puzzled and concerned. An answer to her question rose up deep within me. "You are called to make known the manifold wisdom of God in the midst of your suffering."

What I saw was that I could demonstrate and prove to be true, God's grace—His divine enablement in my situation. It was only by His grace that I as a single mother could face and overcome such enormous difficulties. It was only by His grace that I could keep putting one foot in front of another. It was only by His grace that I could be more than a conqueror. It was only by His grace that I could continue my missionary work in spite of the obstacles I had in my family life. Like Paul, I had a thorn in the flesh and the Lord had said to me, "My grace is sufficient for thee."

Since I have come to understand our calling to "make known the manifold wisdom of God," I have been able to go through trials and tribulations with a different perspective. There is a purpose behind my suffering and I have an awesome privilege to demonstrate, by my response, different aspects of what God accomplished in Christ Jesus at the cross. I am reminded of a woman who witnessed her parents being shot and killed by a young man when she was 8 years old. Years later she forgave the man and even spoke to him face to face. She was demonstrating and making known another aspect of God's grace, His forgiveness. He forgave us when we were undeserving and she extended the same grace to her parents' killer.

I often think of Martin Luther and the reformers who continued to make known the truth of the gospel, that we are justified by faith without the works of the law, in spite of great suffering. They were threatened with imprisonment, death, persecution, false accusations and loss of property. In fact, Martin Luther was hesitant to marry because of the danger he faced from evil forces.

As Luther and others preached the truth of justification by faith and worshipped with the truth, they were demonstrating and displaying an important aspect of the redemption of Jesus Christ to principalities and powers over their region. Their willingness to suffer for the truth and to live out the truth in the midst of trials and tribulations affected the prevailing knowledge of that day and brought Europe out of the Dark Ages.

No one wants to experience suffering. However, we live in a fallen world marred by sin and ruled by the evil one. We live in a battle zone and like Job we are often unaware that our battles not only take place in this realm, but also in the heavenly realms. We do not realize the important part we play in the eternal scheme of things. Principalities and powers rule over areas with incorrect knowledge, the knowledge of the kingdom of Satan. But we as individuals and as the church can make known through our daily walk and responses the manifold wisdom of God.

We have an opportunity to display everything that God accomplished in Christ Jesus as we continue to trust and love God in the midst of our sufferings. We have an awesome opportunity to demonstrate His love, His grace and His victory. **We have an opportunity to make known the manifold wisdom of God, to display and show to be true all that Christ accomplished at the cross—to penetrate the heavenlies with the knowledge of God.**

A Different Mentality

"Lassie, whatever you do be a
good soldier of Jesus Christ."

THESE WERE DR. JAFFRAY'S LAST WORDS TO DARLENE
DIEBLER ROSE BEFORE HE WAS TAKEN BY THE JAPANESE
DURING WORLD WAR II. WORDS WHICH SHE SAID WERE TO
SUSTAIN HER DURING THE AWFUL TIMES AHEAD.

"How far we have fallen from a soldier's mentality," I lamented
after studying the biographies of missionaries like Jonathan
Goforth, James Frazier, Hudson Taylor and Dr. Jaffray. A soldier's
mentality cuts across the American way of life. Until recently we
felt it was our right to be blessed, have all our needs and wants met,
be successful, rich and live a life of pleasure, to fulfill the American
dream. And we have had a good life, a life that is envied by the rest
of the world. However, this life can lead to dullness and compla-
cency. We have lost the cutting edge of the early saints. They had
a soldier's mentality.

Paul told Timothy to "endure hardness as a good soldier of Jesus
Christ." A soldier's life is not one of pleasure, comfort and ease. It

is a life of discipline, hardship and at times suffering. A soldier is on call 24/7 and is at the command of the one who has chosen him. A soldier's life does not revolve around himself but around the plans and purposes of his commander. We need a paradigm shift today in our thinking from a blessing mentality to a soldier's mentality. This involves changing our attitude towards suffering.

There was a turning point in my life when I began to look at suffering with different eyes. I was reading Madame Guyon's autobiography. I marveled at her attitude towards suffering and her submission to God's will in the midst of it. She wrote, "God kept me in such a disposition of sacrifice, that I was quite resigned to suffer everything, and to receive from His hand all that might befall me, since for me to offer in any way to vindicate myself, would be only beating the air." My response to adversity was not like hers. By this time, I had experienced my share of suffering, but my reaction was more like a dog licking his wounds.

When I finished reading her book, I entered into a time of prayer, the kind of prayer that can only be led by the Holy Spirit. I do not remember the exact words but the essence of the prayer was asking God to do a deep work in me. Had I known that in a few days I would be facing the kind of suffering no woman wants to experience—the death of her husband—I might not have prayed that prayer.

Three years later the Lord challenged me to take seriously a soldier's mentality. Would I embrace all that was involved in being a soldier of Jesus Christ? As I searched the scriptures I found that Paul expressed the heart of a soldier when his friends begged him not to go to Jerusalem where tribulations awaited him. "And now behold I go bound in the spirit unto Jerusalem, not knowing the things that shall befall me there. Save that the Holy Spirit witnesses in every city, saying that bonds and afflictions abide me." But none of these things move me, neither do I count my life dear unto myself so that I may finish my course with joy, and the ministry, which I have received of the Lord Jesus to testify the gospel of the grace of God"(Acts 20:24). These words of Paul were quickened to Madame Guyon as she traveled toward France where persecution and great suffering awaited her.

I noticed a common thread as I studied the lives of missionaries and well-known saints. They all experienced suffering but continued to fight the good fight of faith. They had a soldier's mentality. Amy Carmichael, missionary to India, fell into a hole crippling her for the rest of her life. This tragedy did not stop her for she wrote many books during those trying years. Hudson Taylor did not let the loss of three children, his wife at age 33, and the death of many of his missionaries in the Boxer rebellion, keep him from bringing the gospel to China. E. M. Bounds suffered imprisonment during the Civil War, banishment from his homeland, and danger as he ministered to men in the midst of the battle. Yet, he persevered in prayer and the preaching of the Word and saw revival break out among the troops. Then there was Corrie Ten Boom, who lost several family members during World War II and endured the torment of a Nazi prison camp. She did not let bitterness stop her, but went around the world testifying to the forgiveness and love of God.

The soldier's mentality which these saints exhibited was the same as Nehemiah's, when he was asked to meet with his adversaries Sanballat and Tobiah. "I am doing a great work so that I cannot come down: why should the work cease, whilst I leave it and go down to you" (Nehemiah 6:3)? Here we have a picture of a soldier's mentality through Nehemiah. "I won't come down off the wall, I won't stop, I won't quit. If I face a mountain I will go over it, if I can't go over it then I will go around it and if I can't go around it then I will go through it."

The words of Ignatius, an early Christian martyr challenge me, "Now I begin to be a disciple. I care for nothing of visible or invisible things so that I may but win Christ. Let fire and the cross, let the companies of wild beasts, let breaking of bones and tearing of limbs, let the grinding of the whole body, and all the malice of the devil, come upon me; be it so, only may I win Christ Jesus."

I think of a dear friend, Rick Seiver, who recently went to be with the Lord. He was a soldier in Viet Nam when a grenade went off in his hand resulting in serious injuries. He lost his right arm and fragments of the grenade entered his body including his brain causing his left side to be paralyzed. Even though he was in a wheelchair for 40 years, he did not let his disability stop him. He became a powerful intercessor and witness for the Lord. During his last days when his body was racked with pain from cancer, he testified to the love of God in Christ Jesus.

These are all a testimony to me. They are a part of the great cloud of witnesses. Like Paul they are saying, "Fight the good fight of faith. Run the race that is set before you for God is with you." They bear witness to the fact that, ***The sufferings of this present time are not worthy to be compared to the glory that shall be revealed in us" (Romans 8:18).***

"Lord, may we of this generation have the same commitment to you as Ignatius, the same perseverance as Hudson Taylor, and follow Dr. Jaffrey's admonition, "Lassie, whatever you do be a good soldier of Jesus Christ."

For our light affliction, which is
but for a moment, worketh for us
a far more exceeding and eternal
weight of glory; While we look not
at the things which are seen, but
at the things which are not seen:
for the things which are seen are
temporal; but the things which
are not seen are eternal

      —2 CORINTHIANS 4:17, 18